Gaston's Crow's Nest

an Alaska Tale

Marianne Schlegelmilch

PO Box 221974 Anchorage, Alaska 99522-1974
books@publicationconsultants.com
www.publicationconsultants.com

ISBN 978-1-59433-116-9
eBook 978-1-59433-144-2

Library of Congress Catalog Card Number:
200900000

Copyright 2009 by Marianne Schlegelmilch
—First Edition—

This is a work of fiction. All of the characters, organizations, and events portrayed in this novel are either products of the author's imagination or are used fictitiously.

All rights reserved, including the right of
reproduction in any form, or by any mechanical
or electronic means including photocopying or
recording, or by any information storage or
retrieval system, in whole or in part in any
form, and in any case not without the
written permission of the author and publisher.

Manufactured in the United States of America

Dedication

**For
Angie**
To the wonder of life's journey

Acknowledgements

Photography
Bill and Marianne Schlegelmilch

Photo Illustrations
Dick Lowthian

Cover Art
Brian Parker
Swanky Studios, LLC

Editor
Joyce Baker Porte

Contents

Dedication		3
Acknowledgements		5
Prologue		9
Chapter One	Leaving the Nest	11
Chapter Two	Gone Too Soon	19
Chapter Three	One Old Salt and a Few Good Men	27
Chapter Four	Legacy to Destiny	35
Chapter Five	Behind the Emerald Cove	43
Chapter Six	The Gift of Love	49
Chapter Seven	Blessed Hope	55
Chapter Eight	Against All Odds	61
Chapter Nine	Hunkered Down	67
Chapter Ten	Bittersweet	75
Chapter Eleven	Spring	81
Chapter Twelve	Merciful Time	87
Chapter Thirteen	Seattle	91
Chapter Fourteen	The Power of Love	97

Prologue

Buffeted by the deep, silty waters of the sub-arctic estuary known as Cook Inlet, miles of tree-laden sandy cliffs rise to form the shoreline of Alaska's Kenai Peninsula. In these waters of the farthest reaches of the North Pacific, wild salmon make their way home to spawn in the rivers and streams that lace this narrow mass of land.

Jutting south from the mainland of Alaska, the Kenai Peninsula is bordered on one side by Cook Inlet and the other by the Gulf of Alaska. Rising from the eastern side of this peninsula are the Kenai Mountains, home to the Harding and Sargent Ice Fields. Across the peninsula's flat expanses, wind the powerful Kenai, Kasilof, Russian and Anchor Rivers.

Rich with salmon, these rivers support a healthy population of birds, moose, bear and other wildlife, along with the humans who live alongside them.

Ever-present inland in summer and along the abundant coastline in winter, the American eagle, as it is also known, soars majestically in the thermals and currents of this pristine place. Their nests, some easily visible from the lone highway that traverses the peninsula, are a certain reminder that this is a nurturing land spilling with earth's bounty.

Gaston's Crow's Nest is a fictional story set in the early years of the last quarter of the twentieth century when Alaska was still only lightly inhabited, and pioneering lifestyles still prevalent. It is a story of an eagle that begins life's journey in the pristine setting of the Kenai Peninsula. Aboard an Alaska fishing boat, he finds his future entwined with humans and the sea.

It is a story of courage, life challenges and discovery. Mostly, it is a story of coming to terms with the lessons one learns and of finding out who you are.

Chapter One
Leaving the Nest

About May of each year, in the aged cottonwood and old growth trees spread throughout Alaska, fledgling eagles poke their downy heads above the woody edges of their nests. Just as in times before and since, the emergence of nature's young heralds the arrival of spring.

The eagles' nests, some spanning a width of four to eight feet and sometimes equally deep, are used every year by the same mated pair of eagles to lay their eggs and to later care for the two to three chicks that are typically hatched. By summer's end, having become nearly as large as their parents, the young birds will be strong enough to fly away and live alone.

Easily recognizable in the first four years of their life by their mottled brown coloring, the young birds will congregate along salmon rich rivers in summer, and coastal bodies of water in winter as they soar with other eagles to hunt for food.

On the southern Kenai Peninsula, the eagles fly as they always have, spiraling above the area's cliffs, gliding along the Homer Spit, and sitting on rocky outcrops along the shores. Undeterred by either wind or cold, they seem to flourish in the strongest gales as they fly effortlessly, one with the wind, until diving suddenly to grasp a meal of fish or small animals with their powerful talons.

For as long as anyone can remember, seldom has there been a light pole or ship's mast in local harbors that in the winter does not hold a sitting eagle scanning the surroundings. In places with fewer spiked objects to use for perches, the eagles have long been known to tuck themselves into rocky ledges along the cliffs, or atop tall trees or buildings where they can have a clear view of their world.

Hali tightened his talons against the crown of the spruce tree as a single shot rang through the crisp dawn air. His hatch-mate, Leuc, had already flown down to Homer for the winter, but as he had done each of these first three winters of his life, Hali would wait to join him until the snow depth made hunting near the Anchor River too difficult. Fluffing his feathers, he settled into the treetop, lessening the grip his feet had on the top branch and scanning the area for snowshoe hare.

Instead of his favorite meal, he saw an old grizzly boar break out of the brush and run toward the far side of the river. For some reason, the old bear had been late to hibernate for the past two winters, prompting the woman who lived in a cabin nearby to fire her rifle every morning to run it off before taking her dogs outside.

As many times as he had heard the sound, Hali still flinched when the sharp snap pierced the air. Even though he knew where to sit so he was not in the line of fire, the sound frightened him as much as it did the bear, causing him to stay well away from the woman's cabin and other two-legged creatures like her that he occasionally saw along the river.

Now that it was nearly October and the days palpably shorter, hunting was more difficult for eagles like Hali that rely on their keen eyesight to spot prey. As the light peaked around noon, Hali snagged a young hare with his talons and dropped it in a hollow near a downed tree. After eating his fill, he left the rest for the scraggly old boar, tearing it up into tender pieces with his beak for the toothless bruin to finish. The aged once fierce predator had difficulty overtaking game, and Hali instinctively knew that the bear probably wouldn't make it through winter this year. Let him have a bite to eat for now. Hali was young and his eyesight sharp. He would have no trouble finding more food.

The second week of October brought the first big snowfall of the season along the river. Hali hadn't seen the old bear at all over the past week and knew it had probably denned up for the last time. Aside from a human squatter in an old RV parked just off the road where the river came close to the highway, the area was quiet and still. Even the morning rifle shots had stopped. Except for an occasional wolf moving through, there was little activity, prompting Hali to take off for the Homer Spit where there was less snow—at least for now.

Chapter 1—Leaving the Nest

Leuc was waiting for him down by the old dog refuge on the spit. Large for his age, Leuc's head had already begun to turn white, unlike Hali's whose head was still completely brown. Leuc had beautiful, piercing yellow eyes and a magnificent wingspread. He stood out as a fine specimen among the other eagles, and even those who had long dominated the spit paid deference to the young bird.

Leuc and Hali spent the afternoon soaring over the deep-water dock before landing on the dirt parking lot that housed hundreds of boat trailers in the summer. Here, where it was warmer than Anchor Point, the lot was covered in massive puddles of water from the heavy rains that had fallen and soaked the area for the past month. With the temperatures hovering at freezing, a fine layer of ice was beginning to form over the puddles.

Some of the eagles had broken through the ice and stood with their feet immersed in the water. Leuc and Hali found it more interesting to see how far they could walk across the thin layer before falling through. Leuc had mastered a technique for making it halfway across by fluttering his wings before his weight caused one of his talons to poke a hole in the ice. The two brothers spent over an hour skimming the puddles this way, Hali following behind Leuc and the other birds watching. A couple of humans with cameras leaned out of their car window to take pictures of the two, which made the young eagles flap a little more dramatically and splay their talons a little wider as they enjoyed all the attention.

Hali had a gentleness with his beak that stood out from the rest of the eagles. As the two became tired of their game of ice-skipping, he called to Leuc who watched him hoist a perfect square of thin ice nearly as large as his head into the air with his beak without breaking it. Leuc cocked his head sideways, seeing his reflection in the frozen square. Some of the other eagles did likewise before Hali set it down and resumed ice walking with his brother. Near evening, the two joined the other eagles on the spit for a special treat from the lady who loved eagles before nestling into the rocks on the jetty that protected the harbor. There they slept for the night, unbothered by the hammers and bangs made by a hefty fisherman with a limp and his lean, younger assistant who had been working steadily on a boat nearby. And, so the days of October went, as did those of November, then December.

With winter solidly upon the Homer Spit, Hali began yearning for some new adventures. It wasn't that soaring over the pounding, windswept surf wasn't exciting, or that hovering over a crashing wave to snatch a fish caught in the incoming tide didn't amuse him, but Hali was not an eagle who aspired to be simply one of the hundreds of eagles who frequented the area. For him there had to be more. In his estimation, he had not been born with a wingspread of nearly seven feet to simply hover over this narrow land mass for days on end. With wings like he had, Hali felt certain there were bigger currents to fly. Many times he talked to Leuc about the two of them flying off over the water just to see what they could find, but Leuc would have no part of it and told him that their life was there on the spit in the winter and farther up the peninsula in summer.

"There is no more perfect place on earth than this land upon which you were born," Leuc told him. "It is the land of your parents and will be the land of their grandchildren. Put aside your wishful thoughts for impossible dreams, Hali, and look around you at paradise. There is no need to look any further."

After a while, Hali stopped talking to Leuc about his dreams and even tried to stop thinking about them himself as he settled into winter life on the spit. Maybe Leuc was right.

Chapter Two
Gone Too Soon

With the increasing light of late February and early March, come the ravages of nature. Late winter sea storms and gales regularly pound the Homer Spit, often throwing full sized logs and large rocks onto the only road down the narrow five-mile stretch of land that juts into Kachemak Bay. Despite the danger, people persist in driving down the Spit road, trying to dodge the waves crashing over them as they play a game of chance with nature in hopes that the rocks thrown by the sea will not break the windows of their vehicles.

Churning and turbulent, the sea pummels the shore, especially at high tide. Waves, windswept, send bubbles of sea foam tumbling across the road, tear pilings loose from docks, and pack sideways-driven snow into drifts along the beaches. The power of the sea is terrifying, yet in the blasting currents the eagles soar, swooping and darting about with playful abandon. Powerful in flight, they take advantage of the energy of the storms to master the forces of the wind.

Formidable as they are in the air, the eagles are equally as vulnerable in water. Although some have been known to swim, they are generally disadvantaged if their feathers become wet and their bodies cold.

Designed for soaring over large bodies of water, eagles with their powerful talons are better suited to grab prey from the surf than they are to ride the waves themselves. They grab their prey from the water and consume it on the shores, retreating from crashing waves as they eat. During long periods of heavy rains, they sometimes perch on prominences close to the ground with their wings held out slightly to dry, dotting the landscape like feathered triangular statues. Dependent on open bodies of water for the activities of life, they cling to the land when at rest.

The day Leuc drowned was the beginning of the end of Hali's life on the Homer Spit. Even now, months after the accident, the remembrance brought pain to Hali's erstwhile carefree existence. On that fateful day, several boaters had reported a whale tangled in a fishing net just beyond the mouth of one of the rivers on the far side of the Inlet.

After several days of effort, the net had been cut and the whale freed. Unknowingly, a large piece of the net had been lost during the whale rescue. Caught up in the outgoing tide, the loose net had somehow become tangled on one of the large trees that often float in the sea and had been dragged in the currents until washing up near the Homer Spit.

It was during a storm when Leuc soared and dove in the wind that he saw a fish and swooped low to grab it from the water. The fish was already dead and Leuc released it almost as soon as he grabbed it, but not before his talons became entangled in the hidden net that was sloshing against the rocks just under the surface of the angry sea. Unable to retract his talons and free his foot from the net, a large wave, followed in quick succession by two larger ones, pounded him into the water and pulled him under.

Leuc fought valiantly to free himself from the net, and several eagles saw him rise out of the water at least twice but the wind and the surf were too powerful and the current too strong. Leuc, despite the strength of youth, was pulled under and drowned. A couple of humans walking the beach at low tide the next day found him still tangled in the net atop the huge rocks that brace the Spit road from the forces of the sea.

Hali watched the humans gather around Leuc on the beach as a vehicle with an emblem on it's door drove up, loaded Leuc into the truck bed and took him away. Still resplendent in death, Leuc's outstretched wings filled most of the pickup bed and he looked asleep there and at peace. Hali was grateful at least for that as he and the other eagles followed the truck along the spit road until it turned down a city street. From a nearby tree, Hali watched the men unload Leuc and take him inside of a building with the same markings on its side as the truck had on its door. He never saw his brother again.

Most of the eagles stayed away from the rocky parts of the Spit after that, preferring to hunt near the harbor or up along the bluffs above Homer where even in winter small game was abundant. Hali refused to turn away from the sea; instead, he challenged every breaking wave in Leuc's name even when he knew it was dangerous. Some days he flew to the point of exhaustion before finding a place sheltered from the wind in which to rest.

One of his favorite resting spots was the top of a large old boat docked among others of equally large size near the entrance to Homer Harbor. He had already become used to the noisy din of repairs made by the two men below. Here, atop the straight stick mast, Hali slept on the small platform surrounded by vertical metal rods that formed a cage. Secure inside the metal basket that kept him from sliding off as the boat rocked in the harbor, he rested. When he became hungry, he would hunt for food, bringing it back to the platform to enjoy.

Chapter 2—Gone Too Soon

Hali spent most of his leisure time here when he wasn't flying, lazily scanning the harbor and trying not to think about what had happened to Leuc.

A large sea lion that wintered in the harbor offered some diversion, often climbing onto boats to steal fishermen's catch. Hali saw the humans in the same truck that had taken Leuc away gather along the docks and point at the sea lion as they talked.

Several seals also inhabited the harbor, popping their heads up to focus their large, black eyes on the surroundings before diving back into the water. Occasionally, a sea otter would float in, lazily pushing himself along with one hind flipper while pounding a clamshell open with a rock on his chest. Despite small icebergs floating with the tides into the protected area, the humans maintained an active presence in the harbor as they moved their boats in and out during the day. The larger boats brought fish to the loading dock for processing while the smaller ones offloaded their fish using coolers that they transferred the fish into and then pulled up the ramps on dollies.

Hali supposed this would now be his life. With Leuc gone he was alone. Having separated from his parents long ago, he was about to enter his fourth year. His eyes had changed from the brown color of youth to the beautiful bright yellow of adulthood, and aside from a few remaining brown feathers; most of his head and tail feathers had turned the white color of maturity.

As the days grew longer and the air began to

warm, he began to venture away from the harbor more often. When he did, it felt invigorating. It was good to again feel the freedom that came with soaring over the bay. Before long he was spending more time away from the boat than he was on it, returning mostly at night to sleep. Sometimes he flew out and landed on the masts of some of the large ships that put down anchor in the bay as they sought shelter from storms farther out at sea. These ships were a good place to spot fish

and sometimes members of the ship's crew would sneak him some leftovers from their dinner when they knew the captain wasn't looking, ignoring the law against feeding the eagles. These men often looked different than the ones Hali encountered in Homer. They had a voice that sounded different from those he had heard during his short life there and their clothes and faces looked different, too.

Chapter 2—Gone Too Soon

All these ships had large flags flying from the masts that Hali like to perch on, but the flags were not like those he was used to seeing around Homer.

Intrigued by the big ships and curious about the people that lived on them, Hali eagerly visited each new vessel that came into the bay. Apparently the ships were a popular destination for birds, because hundreds of seabirds of varying species hung around them. Many of these birds hunted differently than Hali did, preferring to fly around in huge, tightly synchronized flocks; their silvery wings catching the sun as they moved as a unit above the sea.

Of course, there were the gulls. Hali had learned that they were just about everywhere in his world. He found them to be opportunistic and somewhat pesky. Sometimes they tried to chase him. Just for fun he played along, letting them think they really could catch him. After a while, tiring of the silly game, he ignored them.

There were other birds out near the ships as well; medium-sized black and white ones with huge orange beaks. Hali watched them sometimes as they dove deep into the water where they would stay for several minutes before coming up. It scared him when they did that. It reminded him of Leuc. As far as Hali was concerned, if the water could overcome someone as magnificent as Leuc, then how could these fat little birds with the beaks that made them top heavy survive?

He screeched at them, extending his neck outward and raising his beak to the sky, opening his mouth to let out a staccato burst of high-pitched squeals. Not understanding eaglecry, the diving birds ignored him and went about hunting in this way that was so foreign to Hali.

Eventually, Hali got used to watching them dive and could see that they were well equipped for the job. Not bogged down like he was with the massive wingspread that allowed him to easily fly at speeds of thirty-five miles per hour, these small birds had tight, water-resistant feathers, webbed feet, and wings that worked more efficiently in water than they did in the air. How interesting this world at sea, where so many things were different from Hali's life in Homer.

For the next several months, he studied the ships and the other birds, mixing his studies with his day-to-day life on the spit. In spite of what Leuc had told him, there was a great big world beyond the one he had been born into. Although he didn't know how and he didn't know when, he knew that one day he would leave Homer to go out and see what he could see.

"I loved you so much, Leuc, my brother," Hali called into the wind. "You lived a magnificent life in your short time on earth, but for me, I must go out and find my own way."

Hali spread his wings and soared above the harbor before landing in the crow's nest that had become his home.

"You will always be with me, Leuc. Send me your spirit. Send it to help guide me and keep me safe and strong."

Chapter Three
One Old Salt and A Few Good Men

With the emergence of spring, longer days and warmer nights come to the Kenai Peninsula. Gradually melting, the snow sinks, first into a deep slushy heap, and then into puddles of water that give fresh glimpses of the ground underneath. Receding snow berms, with their crusty toppings of road grime, dot the edges of the parking lots and roads. By the beginning of May, the snow is gone and the first salmon of the season begin to arrive from their long ocean's journey. The salmon move first to coastlines near the rivers of their birth after returning from the farthest reaches of the sea, and, then, upriver in their final journey. With the last life within them, they lay their eggs in the place they were born and then they die, leaving the river and the sea to the next generation.

While motorists struggle to navigate the pothole-ridden highways of this period known in Alaska as breakup, the fishermen of the southern Kenai Peninsula begin to move their boats in and out of the harbor, taking them out on the fishing expeditions that earn them a living. By the time exasperation with road conditions has reached its peak, seemingly overnight the highways return to their usual dry and dusty state of normalcy.

Gaston's Crow's Nest

Early-bird recreational boaters also begin to arrive. Launching their boats into the protected waters of the harbor and tying them up near dock space they have rented for the upcoming season, they turn the harbor parking lot into a mass of empty boat trailers. Tour boats, fishing charter boats, and water taxis also become more evident as spring emerges—a sure sign that summer is near.

Along the Homer Spit Road, merchants unboard the windows of their small shops, and freshen the weathered exteriors with new coats of paint. Boardwalk platforms set on pilings driven into the beach hold an eclectic array of shops. Soon they will host the circus of visitors camped in tents, RV's and boats along the spit, replacing the sleepy pace of winter with the frenzied fury of a short Alaska summer.

Some of the professional fishermen use this time to prepare their boats for the coming long summer at sea. Working the season from fishery to fishery, they will offload their catch onto commercial tenders that meet them in the fishing grounds and from which the fish will be taken to market. In the Homer Harbor, one such fisherman worked earnestly on his seiner, the Angelina.

Gaston Angelo Noel limped down the floating dock to the dark blue seiner tied along the outer t-span of wooden walkway that made up the first section of the Homer docks. Hurling a canvas duffel bag that was almost as large as he was up over the deck rail, he bent to pick up a tube of toothpaste that had fallen out of the bag when he threw it, grabbing his left knee with both hands and wincing with pain as he stood up.

How tired he looked as he held onto his leg before straightening his back and tossing the toothpaste over the rail in the direction of the duffel bag. Grabbing a rope that dangled from the deck rail, he stepped onto the plywood platform next to his boat and hoisted himself aboard.

Out of breath from the effort, he eased his burly frame into something between a leaning and a sitting position on the deck of his seiner and stroked his graying beard with one hand as he thought about the surgery that he would soon need to repair his damaged knee. A whoosh of air and a streak of black feathers startled him and almost caused him to lose his balance and fall.

"What in the name o'…Geezo Pete…" he sputtered while ducking.

Peeking through the elbow crook of the arm he had raised to protect his face from the feathery missile, he saw an eagle sitting above him in the crow's nest of his boat.

Hali chose that moment to unceremoniously lean forward, lift his tail feathers, and squirt the remnants of this morning's breakfast onto Gaston's rear deck, just missing the duffel bag that lay in the center of the floor.

Gaston eased himself up, limped the few feet to the bag that held all his belongings, and dragged the duffel bag closer to him, ignoring the bird. Years spent living in eagle habitat had taught him that it was more trouble than not to convince officials that a person was not harassing the official bird of the nation, even if the harassment was the other way around. Hali looked down, hopped a half turn inside the crow's nest, and closed his eyes.

"Yeah, it's the same danged bird," Gaston complained to one of the crewmembers who had come out of the galley to see what all the commotion was. "I remember seeing that white patch on his leg feathers the last time he was here."

Gaston leaned over the deck rail and spat into the water before wiping his arm across his mouth and continuing, "If I didn't use that crow's nest so much, I'd yank 'er down just to keep the birds outta here."

"I can get rid of 'im, Cap'n," the crewman said.

"Won't do no good, Eel. He'll just be back right after," Gaston sputtered.

"Help me with this bag here, would ya…"

Used to the noises of boat's engines and the rocking wake created by their comings and goings, Hali slept, giving little notice to the disturbances that had by now become familiar. Only hours later did he realize that he was no longer in Homer. Not only was he not in the harbor, but he was no longer anywhere near the Kenai Peninsula. Fluffing his feathers before hopping atop the edge of the cage that formed the crow's nest, he gripped the white paint-chipped metal with his feet and looked around.

He saw land not far in the distance—a cone-

Chapter 3— One Old Salt and a Few Good Men

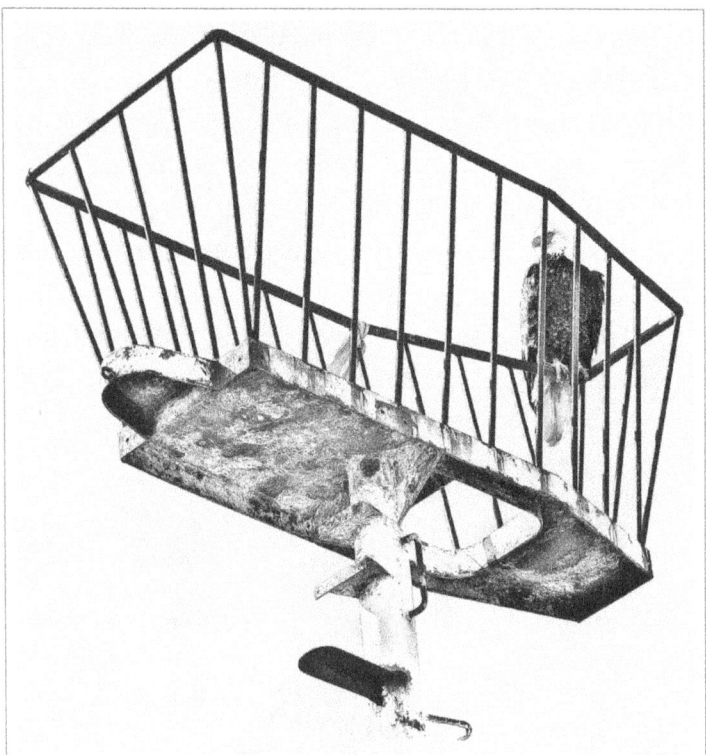

shaped mountain rising out of the sea with steam coming out its top. This was not familiar land, but he was hungry, so he lifted his wings and flew off towards the mountain. Rumbling and shaking from the giant cone turned him back. Worse than the shots that used to wake him every morning in Anchor Point, these sounds made him nervous, so he flew back to Gaston's seiner, swooping low to snatch a fish from the sea as he did. A couple of gulls tailed him and tried to grab his fish from the floor of the crow's nest, but Hali spread his wings over the lifeless fish and ate his fill. Only then did he fly out in search of another, leaving the carcass to the gulls.

As this scene repeated itself over the next several days, the *Angelina* chugged steadily out to sea. On the third day, Gaston guided his seiner into a spot close to shore, briefly awakening his crew long enough to set anchor and prepare for the next day's fishing. A short night later, he and his men ate breakfast prepared by a greenhorn deckhand hired for this season, and waited their turn to drop the nets into the water.

Hali took the opportunity to explore his surroundings. Staying well away from the steaming mountain, he flew above the emerald bluffs and cliffs that rose from the turquoise water, even meeting a couple of other eagles as he did. For a while he perched on one of the spruce trees, where his now fully white head stood out like a holiday ornament along the shore, and watched Eel show the greenhorn how to stack the nets.

Something about this moment made him think of Leuc. Hali wished his brother could be here with him to experience these new sights and sounds. Even as he knew that Leuc had never desired to leave Homer, Hali held tight to the belief that his brother would have changed his mind had he had the opportunity to see what he was seeing from this tree. He sat there watching the fishing boats pull nets filled with fish from the water. He saw two eagles he hadn't met fly by. Closing his eyes, he napped and dreamed that Leuc was sitting beside him.

Happenstance had brought Hali on this adventure, or so it seemed. Or, perhaps it had been his destiny. Awake now, he flew down to a rock near the shore where he sat in the sun and preened himself while Gaston and Eel lowered the jitney into the water. He watched as Eel pulled the net away from the *Angelina's* rudder while Gaston pulled it steadily around in a circle with the seiner, encouraging the crew each time they pulled up the net to see their catch of fish bubbling inside. Several times Hali flew out to catch a fish of his own, enjoying the freshly caught salmon on one of the beaches nearby.

When Gaston and the winch man worked to pull the filled net out of the water, Hali circled overhead, tempted to grab one of the flopping fish for himself. Visions of Leuc's lifeless body tangled in

a similar net kept him back. He would fish the way eagles naturally fished and give no more thought to sharing Gaston's bounty. He watched Gaston chug over to the tender where he and his crew unloaded their catch before getting back in line for another set.

Although some of the bigger boats offloaded their catch only once a day, Gaston, having a smaller boat, chose to unload his catch after each set of the net. Today he would visit the tender three times before nightfall when the crew would have dinner and turn in early in preparation for the next day's fishing.

As the crew finished watching a movie video and repaired tears in the nets before turning in for the night, Hali positioned himself in the comfort of Gaston's crow's nest and went to sleep.

Chapter Four
Legacy to Destiny

Thanks to the work of dedicated crewmembers and the convenience of tenders, many fishermen spend the greater part of the summer at sea. With several of the crew hired from locations outside of Alaska, the fishing boat becomes a summer home away from home and the crew their family at sea.

Weekly trips to nearby towns keep the boats stocked and allow the crew time to stretch their legs on land while they pick up supplies. With little money to spend, they live on the adventure until the end of the season when the profits from this year's harvest are dispensed as per prior agreement. The money is as good as the work is tedious. For those who take to the sea, working on a fishing boat is the adventure of a lifetime. Lonely and long, the days seem to go on forever, until one day it is fall and the boat returns to port.

Like the many boats that fish in Alaska's waters, the Angelina *and her crew toiled the summer long, fishing mostly for sockeye and pink salmon. At forty-two feet in length, the* Angelina *was small by Alaska standards and thus able to manage with a crew of four. In his younger years, Gaston had managed with three, but his problem knee and his advancing age made him less agile than he had been in his prime. Having amassed a comfortable nest egg, he now fished as much for the love of the sea as he did for the money, making the expense spent on an extra crewmember a matter of personal convenience.*

Eel had been Gaston's skiff man for close to twenty years, having started as a deckhand. Gaston trusted Eel to manage not only his nets and their catch, but also the safety of his boat—both when the nets were in the water and when they were pulling them out. In his opinion, there was no finer man he could have found for the job, a sentiment Eel shared about his captain.

Each season they hired a young deckhand from the many who sought work on the boats, after which they would spend about two weeks teaching him the job. Only once had they been disappointed when a promising young man from California ended up being more trouble than he was worth. Endangering Gaston, Eel, the boat, and others nearby with his propensity for focusing on everything but the job at hand, they had dropped him off at the nearest port with a one way ticket home. The delay in finding a new deckhand and training him in the middle of the season had cost Gaston thousands of dollars—money that he sheared off his own salary so that Eel would not be left short of the cash needed with which to support his wife and their three children.

Thus Gaston had spent the last forty years at sea. This season, he told himself, would be his last.

Soaring high above the bluffs with only the sky

Chapter 4—Legacy to Destiny

above her, the beautiful eagle known as Lyra spiraled upward as Hali watched her in flight. With her wings slightly arched, the tips of her feathers upturned, she was graceful beyond any bird Hali had ever seen. Caught in the sunlight, her black feathers took on eloquent shades of soft blue, green and gold that defined each graceful wave of her flight.

Watching Lyra reminded Hali of sounds he had sometimes heard coming from Gaston's cabin, sounds Hali had heard Gaston refer to as *Puccini*. Hali would soar to the sounds called *Puccini* as they resonated across the open waters of southern Alaska on those days that Gaston chose to crank up the volume on his battery operated CD player, but he was sure he had never soared with the same grace and beauty as Lyra. Sitting in the crow's nest of the *Angelina,* Hali watched until Lyra rose out of sight.

Gaston churned up the engine on the *Angelina* and began heading away from shore. Impulsively, Hali flew to the bluff where he found Lyra sitting on top of the tallest spruce tree there. The two eagles locked eyes, sharing the unspoken language of the heart, lingering as long as was possible before Hali flew back to the boat that sailed out of sight of this place he had come to know as the Emerald Cove.

For the next month, Gaston fished far from the Emerald Cove. Twelve other boats fished within range of the tender that had been dispatched to the area. Along with the other boats, Gaston and his crew enjoyed a record catch. It had taken Gaston two days to reach the new fishing grounds and to Hali it was almost as beautiful as the last one, but much noisier.

One day, sitting in the crow's nest watching Eel pull the edge of the net down with the skiff to let a sea lion escape, Hali thought of Leuc again. He remembered the day a sea lion had swum into Homer Harbor and the commotion it had caused as officials tried to get it to leave while boaters dodged its repeated attempts to jump onto the back of their boats. He and Leuc had spent the day perched on one of the tall light poles that surround the harbor, and talked in their native language of eaglecry about what a strange creature this was, and how it looked like a giant seal with a head like that of a dog. Much to the consternation of everyone connected with the harbor, the sea lion swam in and out with the tides for the next two weeks before finally swimming off, leaving everyone concerned ecstatic that they did not have to ward off the errant mammal.

"He's one of us," Leuc had told Hali.

"What do you mean, Leuc? He's a mammal—like a seal," Hali responded.

"Protected," Leuc had answered simply. "Some of us are protected from the people who used to hunt us until we were almost gone from the earth."

"I didn't know," Hali responded, leaning down to pick off a piece of grass stuck on his talons and watching it drift to the ground far below.

"Always be careful," Leuc had warned him. "Those who walk on two legs—the ones they call *people*—always be careful and stay back; some of them want to hurt those like us."

Hali thought about Gaston and Eel and the words spoken by Leuc as the sun warmed the crow's nest early one day. He had lived in the crow's nest of Gaston's boat for the better part of the summer. Just as Leuc had been wrong about the wonder of going far away, Hali decided Leuc had also been wrong about people. Neither Gaston nor Eel paid him any mind. Sometimes, one or the other of them would even throw out one of the fish they had caught, knowing that it was within his reach. How he wished Leuc could be here now, learning, as he was, that not all people were bad and enjoying this adventure with him.

Gaston's Crow's Nest

A sharp snap broke the stillness of the morning. Hali recognized the sound just as a bullet ricocheted off the metal rail of the crow's nest, barely missing him. The fright sent him aloft with two powerful flaps of his wings as another shot sent a second bullet whizzing past just inches below his feet. Gaston stuck his head out of the *Angelina's* cabin, holding a rifle with a scope on top.

"I'll give ya till the count o' five to turn that raggedy bucket you're in around, before I fill her so full o' holes, you'll be walkin' on the backs o' whatever salmon happens to be swimmin' by, to save yerselves from drownin'," Gaston assured the two bawdy young men who were circling his boat in an outboard motor powered inflatable raft.

"Jest tryin' to help ya get ridda a pesky eagle," one of them laughed, tossing a beer can in the air and shooting two holes in it before it landed in the water. "Yer not gonna report us, are ya?"

Gaston stepped fully outside the cabin door, raised his rifle to his shoulder and squinted through the scope and barked, "One! ... Two! ... ."

The men slowly circled in the skiff, swigging big gulps of beer from cans and then flinging them into the water. Gaston re-positioned the rifle and pulled the stock more tightly into his shoulder.

"Three! ... Four!" Gaston counted off as the two men in the skiff kept circling. They continued to taunt Gaston as they advanced, coming dangerously close to his boat with each widening circle of their skiff.

"Last warning!" he called. "Five!"

Squeezing the trigger, Gaston fired a warning shot way over their heads, followed closely by a second one a little lower. He briefly lowered the rifle, then raised it again and followed the movement of the skiff through the sight.

"I ain't gonna mess with ya scumbags!" he warned with a bellow, prompting the two young men to defiantly rev their engine and power around in a circle before roaring off just as Gaston fired two more shots in their direction.

"You don't know who your messin' with…" Gaston heard one of them holler.

The *Angelina* rocked in their choppy wake. Soaring overhead, Hali watched, afraid to come back down. He flew like that for a while before finally coming back to the boat and landing gingerly on the edge of the crow's nest.

"They won't be back," Gaston said, tossing a fish up Hali's way before turning back into the cabin and shutting the door.

The coming days proved that Gaston had been right. The two men never returned for the rest of the month that Gaston and his crew fished in the area. Hali heard Gaston tell Eel one morning that the Coast Guard had picked the two young men up and taken them to the Kodiak Jail for endangering wildlife and for misconduct with a weapon among other charges, after he had radioed in their description. Even though it looked like Leuc had been right about humans, Hali knew that Gaston,

Eel and their crew at least, were people he could trust. And so, with each day's end, Hali slept in his usual place in the crow's nest, missing Leuc and dreaming of soaring with Lyra.

As summer drew to a close, the days started becoming shorter and the nights cooler. Gaston's knee was bothering him enough with the colder weather that he now mostly sat on the deck rail calling orders to the two crewmen, while Eel manned the skiff. In early September, Gaston announced that the season was just about over and turned the *Angelina* back towards Homer.

The seas were choppier now than they had been in the long sunny days of summer, and there was more fog. Like Gaston, Eel and the deckhands, Hali sensed it was time to go home before winter set in. When they reached the area Hali knew as the Emerald Cove, Gaston put down anchor for the night and Hali took the opportunity to fly over to the bluff in search of Lyra. When she was nowhere to be found, he returned to the crow's nest and slept, while the *Angelina*, with Gaston and crew in the cabin, rocked gently on the calmest seas of the season.

Chapter Five
Behind The Emerald Cove

Often, along with the dense, moisture-laden air known as fog, come the calmest seas. As if in a misty heaven, the earth dons an ethereal cloak—secure, comforting and protecting. The sea, bathed in the misty air, is calm and silken. The trees, intensely vivid, stand exposed through the haze. Air that has been warm becomes cool, and coolness that has prevailed becomes warm, all depending on which time of year the fog appears.

Comforting to some, disconcerting to others, the fog brings an aloneness that can be viewed as either a precious private moment with the earth—an intimate serenity, if you will—or to some, a claustrophobic uncertainty. Insidiously it creeps across the sea to the land before evaporating into the sun it has veiled from the earth. With the fog comes stillness and peace and when it is gone, a new clarity to all it has touched.

There is nothing quite like the sea when it flutters like a silken cloth under the fog. Seemingly timeless, the silken sea-borne cloud soothes the earth until, wrestled by the wind, it is gone. Crashing waves brought by intruding storms, bring with them foamy currents and rolling swells that rumple the peaceful sea. The contrast, humbling in its magnitude, brings with it wonder—as if all that has gone before, never was.

Hali's downiest feathers rustled with the first hint of the oncoming force, wakening him from a deep sleep and leaving him momentarily disoriented in the heavy fog. The sound of Gaston's snores coming from the deck below, reminded him that he was in his usual place in the boat's crow's nest, although, unable to see through the thick air, he had no idea exactly where they were. His last recollection before falling asleep had been that they were back near the Emerald Cove, which gave him no reason to doubt that was where they had anchored for the night. Shifting himself around in the crow's nest, he hopped up onto its rail before jumping back down. Its flat, round platform had become his home away from home. Secure, he tucked his head down for more sleep. Before he could resume his dream of flying with Leuc over the Homer Spit, an unsettling chop chop of waves splashing against the sides of the boat wrenched him fully awake.

The sound of Gaston stepping out of the cabin down below was a familiar one. Hali knew it was Gaston by the way he banged the door against the cabin before rattling the tin cups out of the cupboard to use for the morning's coffee.

"Thick as pea soup, ain't she Cap'n?" Eel's voice, amplified by the fog, boomed out.

"Better make sure we…" the rest of Gaston's

Chapter 5—Behind the Emerald Cove

words became muffled as the two men walked back inside the cabin.

Moments later the two deck hands came out and made sure the skiff was securely tethered to the side of the boat, securing it with ropes before going back inside.

Hali heard one of the last of the silver salmon from this year's run jump from the water near the boat. He swooped down to snatch it and dropped in onto the deck in front of the galley door, shooting down to grab a second one for himself. Seconds after the freshly killed salmon landed with a thump on the deck, Eel came out to retrieve it and take it inside. Hali had become faithful at sharing his bounty with the men. At first amazed by this unusual behavior, they had come to appreciate the fresh fish that appeared for them each day. It kept them from having to wait to retrieve one from the nets when they dropped their catch off at the tender.

The fish was good. Fresh and tasty, it sated Hali's appetite much in the same way it did that of the four men who enjoyed the one dropped to them by their resident eagle. Hali stayed in the crow's nest, listening to the familiar sounds in the cabin below. The rattle of pots and pans, followed by a discussion of the map Gaston insisted on using— even in these days of the GPS— were what Hali had become used to over the summer.

Normally he would have flown off by now, but he couldn't see beyond the edge of the boat and there were no calls from other birds to tell him in which direction was the land. Aside from Gaston and his men, and the accelerating chop of the waves against the boat, the air was eerily still. The two deckhands had just checked the anchor in front and put down a second one in the rear when the wind began. With a minimum of warning it barreled down on the *Angelina*, and lashed the heavy wooden boat and all aboard with the full fury of the sea.

Hali suddenly slid across the platform in the crow's nest. He clamped his talons around one of the vertical metal bars to hang on. Used to high winds in flight, he felt the air rush through his feathers as he sat powerlessly grounded and unable to steel himself against the onslaught. Just when he thought he could stand it no more, one of Gaston's men climbed up and threw a blue poly-tarp around the cage, wrapping a piece of rope over and around to hold it in place before scurrying back down the mast and back into the cabin. The tarp was enough to provide some shelter from the wind and Hali released the grip his talons had on the metal cage.

The fog, blown out by the wind, was replaced by sea spray and driving rain that, along with the wind, pummeled the *Angelina* and her crew. Hali could see through an opening in the tarp that they had tied up close to a tall spire of rocky cliff that jutted from the sea about fifty yards from shore. If his memory served him correctly, the *Angelina* was anchored on the back side of the cliffs that formed the Emerald Cove.

A sharp crack sent one of the giant spruce trees

sheared off by the wind tumbling down the cliffs into the sea. Two other trees broke in the gale-force winds, but remained partly attached to their base.

Hali tucked his head under his wing and tried to shut out the sounds of the storm. The *Angelina* pitched and rolled as enormous waves began to crash over her sides. In seemingly slow motion, one of them tore her from her rear anchor and whipped her around against the rocks, causing a gaping hole in her side. As water poured onto the deck, Gaston and his men wrestled the cabin door open. They had already stepped into their survival suits when the storm began. Now they frantically pulled them the rest of the way up over their shoulders and heads, and did their best to zip them tightly as they fought the wind.

There was no time to unhook the skiff before the *Angelina's* bow stood upright in the water, pitching Gaston, Eel and the two deckhands into the icy sea. Hali seized the moment before the boat sank to fly sideways under the wind-freed tarp out of the crow's nest. The wind caught his wings and began to carry him away from land. With every bit of strength he had, he flapped his enormous wings and moved against the wind toward shore, where he managed to find a small depression in the rocks that offered him some protection.

When the storm ended the next morning, the *Angelina* and two of her crew were gone. Lying motionless on the beach, still in their survival suits, were Gaston and Eel.

Chapter Six
The Gift of Love

Whipped into a tempestuous fury, sea storms arrive with little warning and when they are spent, retreat as if swept away in silence. Strewn with water-soaked planks and trees, freshly washed beaches sculpted by the pounding waves await the next tide. The water, placid, flat and serene shows no sign of the tempest now blown out. The icy blast, driven into infinity by the sun, no longer holds the earth in its frozen grip.

For the few who survive such an onslaught at sea, the memories of the storm remain to haunt them for the rest of their days. Some will try to forget by dulling their senses with substances and rituals. Others will sleep fitfully, never again to enjoy peaceful slumber. A few of the toughest will return to the sea and defy its attempt to suppress their existence.

Their families will know no peace until they hold their loved ones in their arms at the end of each ocean journey. Silently pleading as they watch them board the boats, their eyes will urge consideration of another way of life just as their voices wish them well. With a brave face, they will launch the seafaring one who is their life's breath on another voyage and pray for their returning embrace.

> *In the sun, on the sculpted post-storm beaches, lie the remnants of that which survives the storm. Objects that have been battered, tossed, whirled and slammed to the shore now give rise to the present.*

The heat of the sun comforted Gaston as he opened his eyes to the brightness of the day overhead, isolated gray clouds whisked across the deep blue sky, remnants of the departing storm. Confused, he forced his aching head to turn from side to side and look about. His neck felt stiff and sore. When he tried to turn his head too quickly, he saw stars. Raising the arms that felt like they were strapped to the earth, he looked at the claw-like mitts that were his hands still encased in his gray survival suit.

"Eel…" Had the word even squeaked out of his parched throat?

"Eel! You okay?" He gasped out with all the strength he could summon before letting his head fall back against the gravel on the beach.

There was no response. With all he had, he lifted his head and called out again, "Eel! You there?"

He heard a moan from beside a rock several feet from where he lay.

"Eel!" Gaston demanded. "Eel! That you? You okay?"

Several agonizing moans later came the words that brought the only relief Gaston wished for at the moment, "I'm… okay… Cap'n".

Reaching up, Eel grabbed the rock with his own neoprene-encased hands and pulled himself to a sitting position. He wiped the back of one arm across his forehead and felt the blood begin to trickle from the freshly re-opened gash that ran from the bridge of his nose to just above his right temple. He tried to steady himself while wresting his upper body from the survival suit, but dizziness forced him down. When he came to again, the sun was on the other side of the sky and Gaston had managed to crawl on his stomach to within inches of his feet, where he now struggled to get his arms out of his survival suit. Eel fought the wooziness that had returned as he sat up again, but managed to push his own suit down below his hips, easing his legs out one by one. He noticed that his clothes were surprisingly dry as he crawled to Gaston to help him out of his suit.

"She's gone," He said, flopping, exhausted, back onto the beach. "She was all the way under by the time we started swimming out of her wake. Didn't think we'd make it…" Eel's voice trailed off.

Gaston stared at Eel, his gaze empty and bewildered. Eel forced himself upright again, blinking his eyes as he struggled to focus.

"Cap'n…" he said gently, "Gaston…" the words did not want to come. "The *Angelina*… She's… Cap'n… the *Angelina*'s gone."

Gaston raised himself on one elbow and stared in a foggy haze at his friend. Slowly, Eel's words began to sink in. Pushing himself to a sitting position, he stared at the sea that now lapped gently at the shore. A blue polytarp, still wrapped with the yellow rope he carried for emergencies, lay crumpled against a rock. Two planks teetered against a sun-bleached tree root that had washed ashore. One of them bore the letters *ANGEL* …the rest of her name gone with the splintered remains of his seiner's third-from-the-top starboard prow board.

"The two greenhorns…" Eel continued, "they're gone, too."

Gaston lay back down, as Eel's words became a distant mumble against his racing mind, "I got the locator beacon activated and a distress signal off just as we went over, Cap'n. They should be out lookin' for us right now."

Closing his eyes, Gaston fought to block out the pain.

It took Hali half a day to find Gaston and Eel. He had flown inland as far as he could to get away from the horrible storm. It hadn't been long before he recognized the area as a small inlet behind the rocks that formed the Emerald Cove. The men had been lucky to have been washed up in this sheltered area where a small crescent of land just above the high tide line kept them safe from both the sea and from the bears that were unable to navigate the sheer cliffs that rose behind them.

Lyra had found the storm-battered Hali hunkered in a hollow in the bluff. She recognized him from the time, weeks ago, when they had spoken with their eyes. Stretching her wings around his shivering body, she warmed him and offered him a silent comfort from the terror she saw in him as he faced yet another loss—that of the humans he loved—to the sea.

Chapter 6—The Gift of Love

In the warmth of the afternoon sun, she led him back across the jagged rocks to the hidden inlet where Gaston and Eel waited for the help they were not sure would ever come. Landing on the beach beside the men, Hali listened for their breath and watched the slight smile creep across each of their lips as they saw him.

With Lyra's help Hali dragged the blue polytarp, which had washed up against the rocks, so that it was alongside the two men. Eel managed to untangle the yellow rope and unravel the tarp, after which he held one corner tightly while Hali and Lyra grabbed two other corners with their beaks and pulled it flat across the ground. First, Eel rolled onto the thick plastic that would protect them from the dampness of the beach. Gaston followed, grabbing his grossly swollen knee and wincing in pain as he did.

From their place on the tarp, the two men watched Lyra lead Hali to a large depression in a rock not far from where they lay. The two birds drank from the pool of fresh water that had been left there from the rain. Watching the two eagles, Eel crawled to the rock, drinking from it, too. When his thirst was quenched, he filled his rubber boot with water and took it to Gaston to drink.

The pain in his knee immobilized Gaston. Already in need of surgery before the shipwreck, it had been wrenched violently as he washed ashore, and the pain was nearly unbearable, even to someone as seasoned to discomfort as he.

Eel found a bandana in his pocket and tied it around his forehead over the large gash he had sustained in the shipwreck. He hoped it would help to stop the bleeding that had finally decreased to a slight, but annoying constant trickle down his face.

Still dizzy, he willed himself to function and reached for two large sticks he saw lying on the beach. He removed a vest he had on under his jacket, wrapped it around his Captain's knee, laying the branches on each side of the knee and then attaching the rope that had been untangled from the polytarp to hold the branches and the makeshift splint together. The splint seemed to help his friend, allowing him enough comfort to at least crawl around, dragging his leg as he did.

Slowly, Gaston, crawled on his side, and Eel, scooted on his seat for fear of standing and falling from the dizziness. They gathered sticks from the beach, and threw them into a large pile near the tarp. Hali and Lyra brought some, too, until a pile as big as an eagle's nest had been formed.

When Eel lit the pile, using the waterproof matches he always carried, flames rose quickly several feet into the air. Frightened by the fire, Hali and Lyra flew up to the top of the bluff and away from the heat. Eel found a couple of pieces of beef jerky in his jacket pocket and shared them with Gaston. As Hali and Lyra flew back to the Emerald Cove, smoke could be seen rising above its bluffs—but not in time to be seen by the Coast Guard Cutter that had passed by only one hour before.

Chapter Seven
Blessed Hope

Hundreds of shipwrecks occur on oceans throughout the world every year. Alaskans face them with the resignation that they are an unfortunate reality of the harsh environment where many make their living on the sea. In Alaska, weather patterns emerge and fade in hundreds of micro-regions of the enormous arctic and sub-arctic landmass that makes up the forty-ninth of the United States of America. These diverse weather patterns move with a speed that challenges the best efforts of the meteorologists who try to predict them. Despite sophisticated sonars, weather buoys, satellites, graphs and coordinated communications among all levels of local, state and national agencies; every year it seems that at least one vessel is lost to the waters surrounding Alaska.

For Alaskans, it is a matter of responding methodically and quickly to incidents as they occur. With never a shortage of volunteers, rescues at sea are launched with the expertise of both professional rescuers such as the US Coast Guard, and with back-up and the full support of communities and citizens who maintain a state of watchful preparedness for the emergencies that are an inherent part of life in the land known as The Last Frontier.

> *As long as there is hope all efforts toward a rescue are expended, often at great risk to the rescuers themselves. Only when all potential for survival has expired does the scenario change from rescue to that of recovery. Survivors in Alaska are buoyed by the knowledge that if there is any way possible, they will be found. Knowing this, most people experienced in the ways of Alaska carry the necessary supplies and skills to maintain the status quo until they are rescued. Though it is sometimes too late for many and some are—despite the greatest of effort—never found, a few will live to tell their story to others who will listen and learn.*
>
> *And, so it goes in the day-to-day life of the people who live close to the land and the seas that bathe its shores.*

Gaston Angelo Noel was well known to the Harbormaster, the Coast Guard Station commander and to most of the fisherman and dockworkers of Homer and other lower Cook Inlet communities. Although he was also known to frequent the Salty Dawg and other drinking establishments, few knew of his work at the food pantry and the local hospice.

Having come to the area after completing his military service at the age of twenty-four, he had spent his entire adult life fishing these waters and trying to distance himself from the painful memories that two years at war had wrought on his tender heart. Few who knew him were aware of his painful past, and knew only that he had—as he had often said—"paid his duty to his country and done it with honor," and had chosen to pursue his passion for a life at sea.

Married for a scant six months right out of the military, he had since sworn off women, except for the loyal few he had scattered in ports throughout the area and who, to this day, uttered his name with nothing short of pure reverence.

He had turned away from the roguish life that spared him from living as a bitter old salt only when finding the love of a woman named Angelina at the age of thirty-four. Her death from cancer on their third wedding anniversary would mark his last marriage. This he solemnly vowed. It was after losing her that he stopped working for others and purchased his seiner, naming it after the only woman who had ever truly captured his heart.

Lying on the beach, Gaston thought about his beautiful Angelina, her loss to cancer, and now the loss of her namesake to the sea. His knee throbbed as he tried to get the numbness in his foot to go away. Unable to exercise in the way he had been accustomed to in the last few years, his weight had reached an uncomfortable level, which only added to the sense of frustration he felt in dealing with the pain.

Eel, on the other hand, was twenty years younger and as lean and wiry a man as could be found. At six-feet-four inches, his long body and agile ability had earned Jameson Andrew Jones the only name recognized by those he knew—Eel.

Married since the age of nineteen to Ella Jo, the two were the loving parents of eighteen-year-old twin boys, and a sixteen-year-old daughter, Jami-Joelle. Fourteen months after the two had married, their first son, Johnson, had died only a few days after his birth.

Eel and Ella Jo had been devastated when they saw their perfectly formed baby suddenly turn blue and struggle to breathe. It was some consolation for the young couple when they later learned that even immediate specialized medical care would not have helped.

Eel and Ella Jo had both been born in Nanwalek, a small community at the tip of the landmass that holds the Kenai Mountains. They had been sweethearts since he first gave her a Valentine in sixth grade, and they both figured they would remain sweethearts long after they joined each other in the heaven that their faith assured them would be their ultimate and lasting final home.

With the Coast Guard now searching for the distress signal from the *Angelina*, back in Homer several members of Eel's church bustled about, taking care of meals for the family and praying for his and the other men's safe return.

Near dusk, Eel shared the last of his beef jerky with Gaston and crawled one more time to the rock for fresh water for the two of them. He noted with relief that there was still enough fresh water for at least two more days, three if they managed

Chapter 7—The Gift of Love

carefully. He would make it his business to be sure that they did.

Wrapped for the night inside the blue tarp, the two men bundled tightly together for warmth near the fire Eel had stoked moments before. Near sunrise, the sound of a carnal roar jolted them simultaneously awake as they watched a sea lion haul up onto the beach, bask in the rising sun and then slip gingerly back into the water. They huddled back underneath the tarp and waited while a passing cloudburst refilled the rocky depression that held their only fresh water supply, and gave thanks that the rain had not lasted long enough to dampen either the inside of their makeshift shelter or their fire.

Hali and Lyra spent the morning soaring over the Emerald Cove, looking for fish. They caught two and ate them. Then Hali caught another and flew back to the two men on the beach, where he dropped the fish close to them in the way that he had done since sailing out to sea in Gaston's Crow's Nest.

More than grateful, Eel dragged the freshly caught salmon to the water's edge and gutted it before skewering it with a stick and cooking it over the fire. For two days, this scene repeated itself as the men rested and tended the fire that burned vigorously with the help of the sticks that Hali and Lyra picked up from area beaches and dropped next to the blue polytarp that had become home.

On the afternoon of the third day, the distant

sound of a helicopter brought both men to their feet and sent the two eagles into a soaring flight pattern high above the bluffs. Frantically, Gaston and Eel scrambled to gather more wood to throw on the fire, adding a wet log to the mix to create a thick column of smoke that rose straight up, high into the air. As the sound of the chopper drew near, the men took the blue tarp from the beach and held it high above their heads, but the helicopter passed by without stopping.

For the first time, the two stared at each other in silence. A single tear trickled down Gaston's cheek as Eel dragged the tarp back to the place on the beach most sheltered from the wind. Looking at each other, each wanted to speak, but neither seemed able to find the words.

Hali and Lyra had flown off with the passing of the helicopter, leaving Gaston and Eel alone on the beach. They stoked the fire, then wrapped themselves tightly with the blue tarp and slept well in to the next day. What was the point, they silently agreed, in doing anything else?

Chapter Eight
Against All Odds

Despite the apprehension and sense of abandonment sometimes experienced by those who survive disasters in Alaska, rescuers aggressively pursue their search for victims, pressing on out of sight of those who would most desperately hope to confirm their efforts—the victims themselves. Numerous stories exist of survivors reporting rescue vessels passing close without seeing them, only to return hours or days later to find them and take them out of harm's way.

Even in the most extreme weather, every effort is expended to find victims of disasters at sea. Human life, even for those well prepared for the uneventful in the extreme conditions of Alaska, is too fragile to sustain the raw forces of nature for more than a few days. Pushing the limits of their own safety, rescuers do all that is possible to reach these survivors, often endangering their own lives in the process. Still, few who engage in this type of work would have it any other way. They are a special breed of human who defy the risk in order to give survivors every possible chance to return to their homes and families.

In rare instances, they too are lost at sea, joining those whom they seek to rescue in a selfless bond. In

Gaston's Crow's Nest

these cases, no amount of training and no amount of preparation can save them from the fate that destiny has in store. Instruments of the hand of God in their success, they become his heaven-bound children in their failure. No work on earth is more selfless than that of those who risk everything to save their fellow man.

Hali was the first to spot the returning rescue boat. From his place soaring above the bluffs, he spiraled higher and higher, riding a thermal brought on by the intense sun.

Lyra soared just below him, tailed by a couple of gulls that eventually gave up their pursuit of the two much larger birds. Trailing behind the boat and somewhat closer to shore, was a Coast Guard helicopter. When the steady Wup, Wup, Wup of the rotors began to echo in the distance across the water, Hali led Lyra back to the beach where Gaston and Eel were just waking up.

Gaston looked up at the eagles and rubbed his eyes. Silently, he asked Hali to bring him a fish, but instead, Hali began picking branches up off the beach and dropping them into the fire. This went on for several minutes as the two eagles swung down close to the fire, fanning it with their wings each time they flew over.

"Enough, you two pesky birds!" Gaston hollered up, trying to shoo them away by waving his arms. "I'm in no mood to play games right now. Get outta here!"

Hali and Lyra ignored Gaston and kept dropping sticks until the fire was burning hot and the smoke rising in a column several hundred feet above the cliffs. It was then that Eel heard the chopper off in the distance.

"Cap'n…Listen…Do ya hear it?"

"Ain't nothin' ta hear cept'n yer ears playin' tricks on ya, ole friend," Gaston dismissed him with a backward swoosh of his hand.

Limping up the beach to the rock that still held a good supply of fresh water, Gaston drank his fill. Years of sleeping next to the hum of his boat's engine, not to mention two years of combat during the war, had left him hard of hearing—something confirmed by testing done at the VA during his trip up to Anchorage last summer. Although fitted with a pair of state-of-the-art hearing aids at no cost to him, Gaston refused to wear them, complaining inwardly that they were a bother, that anything he needed to hear would be loud enough already, and that the rest didn't matter.

He headed to a stand of brush off to the side, where he disappeared into the bushes and relieved himself, before working his way back down to Eel, who had by now moved down to the tide line. As he stood next to his friend, Gaston saw what he had given up hope of seeing.

The silhouette of an approaching Coast Guard Cutter rose on the horizon and the orange of the accompanying rescue helicopter flickered on the water. Coming in quickly behind the two rescue craft, a massive fog bank had already begun to wash over them as they moved steadily toward the shore.

With no time to waste, Hali swooped down and grabbed a corner of the blue tarp in his talons, lifting quickly in the air with the tarp trailing behind. Lyra followed, snatching the opposite corner with her talons as the two eagles flew in the direction of the boat. The wind picked up and a sudden gust caught the tarp and whipped it around Lyra, causing her weight to pull the two birds downward.

Momentary panic overtook Hali as visions of Leuc tangled in the fishing net flashed through his consciousness. Instinctively he zoomed upward, creating a sudden tension on the enormous sheet of blue plastic. This caused it to unwind, hurling Lyra in a life-saving somersault away from the unfurling blue sheet. Lyra quickly righted herself and flew toward Hali and the trailing tarp. Using her talons to grab the opposite corner, she flew beside him as they let it fly in a flag-like motion behind.

Once within sight of the rescue boat, the two eagles pulled the tarp down low enough to be seen by the watchman who was standing out on the deck. As a second crewman responded to the motions of the first, Hali saw the men point in his direction. He turned around and flew in widening circles away from the boat, trying to lead the rescuers in the direction of Gaston and Eel. Curious as to how the eagles had obtained such a tarp and knowing that four men were lost at sea, the cutter followed. By the time the boat was in plain view of the Emerald Cove, the rescuers were able to spot the fire on the beach and see the two men standing on the shore, their arms waving frantically in the air.

Hali and Lyra dropped the tarp onto the fire and watched the flames suddenly shoot higher. As the rescue helicopter approached the beach, they flew up to the top of the bluff and settled into a sheltered cove that was unaffected by the rotor wash of the approaching aircraft.

Hovering delicately over the tide line, the chopper crew lowered a large mesh basket down to where Gaston and Eel stood. With the fog bank rapidly moving in and no time to send a rescue man down, a man with a bullhorn stood in the open doorway of the chopper, yelling at Gaston and Eel to get in. Without hesitation, Eel climbed over the edge of the basket and reached out his hand to pull Gaston in—tugging with all his might to get his friend over the rail and inside.

Moments later, the two men were lifted off the beach and dragged through the air in the basket to a place over the deck of the rescue boat. There, crewmen grabbed hold of the basket as the chopper hovered overhead, and quickly pulled them out onto the deck before signaling the aircraft to pull the basket up.

No sooner had the helicopter moved away from the boat than an enormous gust of wind pushed the aircraft violently sideways, dangerously close to the bluff. At the same time, the basket swung out wildly, also hitting the bluff and entangling itself in the trees. The pilot, unable to pull the basket free from the trees, lost control of the aircraft which landed on its side in the water with a thud before sinking.

Gaston, Eel and everyone on board watched in horror as the three crew members climbed out the window of the upside of the sinking chopper, jumped into the icy water, and swam frantically away from the vessel. Without time to don survival suits and despite split second attempts to throw life preservers to the men—and even before divers could don their gear, the men disappeared with the chopper into the sea—the rescuers having now become the lost.

Chapter Nine
Hunkered Down

Alaska weather can be as unpredictable as it is harsh. Almost instantaneously, a clear sunny day can become a wind-torn dissonance of events. Such are often the circumstances when boats are lost at sea. Leaving only a trail of debris, unexpected storms take their share of any who happen to be in their path. Those who survive are left to deal with the aftermath of the storm, the loss of their friends and the uncertainty of rescue. The frustration and inability of those providing assistance to reach those in need is as intense as is the effort to save them.

When the rescuer becomes the victim, the wild card of fate is cast upon the game table of life. Such was the case in the rescue of Gaston and Eel. First victims, then survivors, and now victims again—who among us would not wonder why they had been spared at the expense of others?

Caught up in what some Alaskans call the "three-day-sock-me-in," the rescue boat with the survivors aboard, along with the remaining rescue crew, pitched wildly in the sea. Precariously close to the cliffs that formed the Emerald Cove, with visibility near zero and with waves washing over the deck, another struggle for their survival fell underway.

The crew of the Coast Guard Cutter moved quickly to get Gaston and Eel inside the warm cabin. Bundled under layers of blankets in a corner, they listened as the captain calmly issued a Mayday call that belied the terror he felt in knowing that the helicopter crew had been pulled under by the suction of the sinking aircraft and would likely never be found in the deep fjord.

Dangerously close to the cliffs themselves, all available crew members worked feverishly to anchor the boat away from the rock face that rose only one hundred feet away. In a daring maneuver, they put both engines to full throttle and managed to round a bend into a horseshoe-shaped cove where they were able to tie up out of the main force of the wind.

With one anchor fore and one anchor aft, they secured the boat against the brutal forces. They posted two watchmen to keep an eye on the anchors as the tide rose and a radioman to listen for any signal from approaching rescuers. Unknown to them, inside a rock cave directly above where they waited, Hali and Lyra huddled, protected from the wind.

Certain that the two eagles had been lost in the advancing storm and writhing in pain from his throbbing knee, Gaston forced his eyes closed to try to block out the progression of tragedies that had made the last four days the worse he had ever experienced on the sea. Eel said the rosary, repeating the prayers over and over in a barely audible whisper

Chapter 9—Hunkered Down

as his thumb and forefinger moved along the beads he always carried in the special pouch Ella Jo had made for him and that he wore around his neck.

As he drifted in and out of long overdue sleep, visions of Angelina began to appear in Gaston's thoughts. She was wearing the blue dress he had given her for their second anniversary and her long hair cascaded over her shoulders as she leaned towards him. Feeling her hand gently caress his forehead and her lips brush his cheek, she talked to him in soothing, familiar words. The sensation of a softly draped warm cloak secured him. He awoke hours later to find himself still on a cot in the corner of the Coast Guard Cutter cabin. Rubbing the sleep from his eyes, he told himself that the comfort of his Angelina had only been a dream.

"It was more than a dream," Eel insisted, when Gaston described what he had seen in his sleep. "She came to visit. She's watching over you. Believe it, Cap'n—Angelina's always with you. She's one of the angels now."

Gaston closed his eyes, trying to believe that what Eel said was right. The thought gave him peace.

Hali awoke in the morning to find Lyra huddled tightly against him in the corner of the rocky cave that was their shelter. He watched her as she slept, grateful that they had found this place of relative solitude. He thought of Leuc, and how he had been alone when he died in a storm such as this. How lucky he was to have Lyra here with him. If he had followed Leuc's advice and stayed in Homer, he would never have found Lyra. Now far away from his birthplace, his belief was reinforced that home was no guarantee of safety. Leuc's untimely death had proven that. Hali closed his eyes and nestled his beak down into his chest feathers as Lyra stirred beside him. They slept protected from the howling wind and driving rain outside.

Across the tiny cove where the Coast Guard Cutter waited out the storm, and down the coast some thirty miles, a faint but steady blip appeared on the signal screen of a second Coast Guard vessel. Having sought shelter at the first sign of the storm, it waited in a sheltered cove out of the wind.

The radioman twisted several knobs and pushed toggles on the control panel, charting the blips and printing a graph that depicted the location of the signal. Minutes later, the blip disappeared. He turned the knobs frantically and flipped switches as he tried to pick up the signal again, but failed to locate it after several minutes. Modern technology aside, he leaned up to the microphone that rose from the top edge of the instrument panel and spoke steadily into the mike.

"Rescue One, this is Rescue Two. Rescue One, this is Rescue Two. Come in Rescue One. Do you copy?"

After waiting a few minutes, he leaned into the mike again.

"This is United States Coast Guard Rescue Two. Do you copy Rescue One?"

Chapter 9—Hunkered Down

The radioman flipped two switches and leaned forward to speak again when signal blips returned to the screen. Static and squelches spat from the speakers just below the mike as he listened.

"ChhhhhhzzzzzzzzzzzzzzzzzaaarchhhhzzzzzOne, chhhhhhhhhhhhhhzzzzrrrrr Copychhhhhhhhhzzzzzzrrrr...." The static was overwhelming, nearly drowning out what seemed to be a response. Seasoned in such rescues, adrenalin now threatening to leach into his voice, the radioman summoned all his composure and continued:

"Rescue Two to Rescue One..."

As he pulled himself closer to the mike that was fixed with screws and plates to the bridge, his voice broke slightly, "Rescue One...we copy! We hear you!"

He wiped the sweat from his brow before continuing, "Rescue One, this is Rescue Two. We copy. Repeat. Rescue One, Rescue Two copies your call. We are en route to your location."

The radioman tore the graph that displayed the location of the new signal loose from the feeder and handed it to the first mate who hurried down the stairs to the Captain's quarters below. Opening the door to the sound of the brass knocker that pounded him awake from his nap, the captain peered out at the crewman who then thrust the printed graph into his hand as he spoke. Still groggy after having been up all night supervising the security of his boat and crew in the storm, the captain squinted and rubbed his eyes as he stared at the paper he held in his hand.

"Captain! Your presence on the bridge is requested immediately," the first mate spit out. "We think we've found them!"

Captain Harlan Johansen studied the data collected by his crew while climbing up the steep ladder-like stairs that rose from the captain's quarters to the bridge. For several minutes he sifted through the charts, graphs and weather reports from the last twenty-four hours, leaning over periodically to discuss the finer points with Officer of the Deck Hans Lucas. Within minutes of his issuing the command to proceed, Coast Guard Rescue Two was churning its way toward Coast Guard Rescue One. At stake were the lives of Rescue One's distressed crew and the two survivors of the *Angelina*, Gaston and Eel.

Despite the poor visibility wrought by the gale-force winds in the area, a check of the weather satellite and consultation with the National Weather Service projected an end to the storm within the next several hours. Thirty minutes later, as Rescue Two churned steadily across twenty-foot swells toward the distressed vessel, the storm ended as abruptly as it had begun.

Hali and Lyra saw the rescue boat coming towards them and flew down, landing on the deck of Rescue One. Gaston was the first to see the two eagles sitting there.

"So you made it okay, too? He said, opening one eye.

Hali hopped along the deck rail and leaned his head down to pluck a wayward feather from

Chapter 9—Hunkered Down

his leg before shaking all of himself in a ripple of flowing plumage that ran from his head to his tail. Looking directly at Gaston, he narrowed his gaze before flying upward and away from the boat with Lyra following closely behind. Less than a half-hour later Hali returned. Flying in circles over Rescue Two, he led it into the small cove that held Rescue One, its crew and the two survivors.

Chapter Ten
Bittersweet

Often anti-climactic, the recovery and transport of wilderness survivors sometimes becomes lost in the public's awareness after the drama of the initial search and rescue.

Occasionally it becomes necessary for things like weather to clear, once the rescue situation and survivors are deemed stable and before transport can occur. During this time, there is inevitably some new event to capture the attention of the public, thus relegating word on these most recent survivors to yesterday's news.

Although important to the immediate circle of family and friends of both the rescuers and the rescued, safe arrival to one's community can best be described—in many cases—as an anti-climax. Where once survival was at stake, the rescued now return home to try to establish a sense of normalcy to their lives and to deal with the tragedy they have faced. Sometimes, they are forced by life's circumstances, to do it alone.

Hobbled by the double tragedy of the loss of the Angelina *and two of her crew, along with the loss of three rescuers and their helicopter, the two Coast Guard vessels functioning as* Rescue One *and* Rescue Two *slid alongside Homer Harbor and tied up at the deep water dock away from the hectic day-to-day activity.*

Gaston, Eel and the others climbed down the gangway off the deck of Rescue One after being debriefed by officials on board. Ella Jo threw her arms around her husband before kissing him all over his face, and daughter JamiJoelle cried with relief. The twins, Ben and Jess, now men themselves, hugged their father and then stepped back to make room for their pastor and several members of his church to surround Eel.

Eel heartily shook the hand of Fr. John Mac, the man who he had known since childhood as his late father's fishing buddy and the pastor of his church. It comforted him to know that he was here now, just as he had been there for each pivotal moment in his life: his marriage, the death of his first son, the births of his twins and then his daughter, and now his own survival from a catastrophe at sea.

Gaston went through the motions of accepting their welcome before sliding, unnoticed, away from the group. After shaking the hands of his rescuers, he limped down the long pile-born dock to shore where someone had hired a cab to take him home.

Rufer barked a greeting from his place inside a fenced dog kennel in the yard. He jumped up eagerly to lick Gaston's face once the latch was undone.

"Looks like they fed ya good, boy," Gaston told his best friend. "Lucky I left ya home this time."

"Welcome home, Gaston," his next-door neighbor, Bob, said exiting the cabin that Gaston called home. "I lit the woodstove for ya. Figured you'd be wantin' to warm up and there's some fresh wood out by Rufer's kennel. Betty sent some of her stew over for you and said there's more where that came from."

Bob and Betty had been Gaston's neighbors for as long as he had lived in the cabin just off the entry to the spit. They didn't come any better as far as Gaston was concerned and although the two men didn't socialize much, they depended on each other with a steady, unspoken neighborly kinship. It had been that way for as long as Gaston could remember.

"Lost 'er," Gaston said simply as Bob walked away on the well-worn path between their houses; stopping Bob in his tracks.

Stepping back, Bob patted Gaston on the shoulder and nodded his silent acknowledgment about the fate of the *Angelina* before turning to walk home.

Close to two weeks passed before Gaston saw Hali again. He recognized the eagle right away by the white patch on his leg and was surprised to see that the bird apparently now had a mate that looked like the eagle that had landed with Hali on the beach of the Emerald Cove and on the deck of Rescue One.

With no boat to work on, Gaston often spent his days walking the docks and talking to other fisherman, usually declining offers to go out with them on a day's fishing. The insurance work on the *Angelina* was taking up a lot of his time as Gaston did all he could to itemize every bit of his loss. How, though, could you put a price on something that had been your life, your livelihood and your haven? Tedious as was the job, he struggled to complete it.

Eel stopped by several times to check on Gaston and eventually signed on with another boat. At least once a week he brought fresh fish to Gaston's cabin, asking him each time when he was going to come over to dinner with him and Ella Jo. Each week Gaston told him it would be soon, but summer was now half over and *soon* had never come.

Hali and Lyra didn't seem to be around much either, although Gaston swore he saw them sitting on Rufer's kennel more than once. In August, he finally had the knee surgery that he had been putting

off for so long. While sitting on his deck early one morning, he saw Hali and Lyra carrying twigs to the top of an old metal piling that stood about 50 feet up out of the water about another 50 feet offshore.

Over the next several weeks, he watched Lyra sit on the piling while Hali carried sticks and placed them just so. Never before in all the years that he had lived there, had Gaston seen eagles try to build a nest on those pilings. Apparently neither had anyone else and soon there was a steady stream of cars driving by watching the two birds work.

The first major storm in October blew half the emerging nest away and left the rest of it in disarray. A few times, Gaston saw the two eagles try to pull the sticks back tightly in place, but when a second and then a third storm battered the open area that held the new nest, he saw Hali and Lyra no more.

Neither did he see much of Eel or Bob and Betty, choosing, instead, to hunker down in his cabin for the winter and let both his mind and his knee heal.

Chapter Eleven
Spring

When it seems that the winter is endless and the darkness eternal, early morning sunrises return and the road ice gives way to dry dusty pavement once more. Brilliant on the horizon, the sun sneaks above the mountain peaks like a diamond flashing in the light thus fading the brilliant orange morning sky into the blue cloak of spring's new day.

The light, blinding and intense, spurs people to come out of their winter hibernation and begin cleaning up the messes left in the wake of the long winter. One day, seemingly out of nowhere, caravans of pick-ups laden with trash bags, scrap wood and metal and even dried out wreaths and trees—with their holiday ornaments dangling from their lifeless branches—begin their steady trek to the Homer dump.

This activity, duplicated in communities throughout Alaska, brings a simple renewal to life in the far north. As the dump conveyor carries away the gritty remnants of the winter, spring emerges to replenish the earth and the people who inhabit its space.

Gaston wasn't sure his old Ford pick-up would make it up Baycrest Hill too many more times.

It had served him well, like a steady friend, but now the rusted fender skirts and battered tailgate foretold the nearness of its last days.

Letting the tailgate drop with a bang, Gaston threw several garbage bags of accumulated household trash onto the dump conveyor before pulling a couple of rolls of chicken wire with dry-rotted wood support strips still attached out of the truck bed. He had meant to clean his yard out last fall, but the sinking of his boat and the surgery on his knee had left him little time or inclination to tackle the removal of Rufer's old dog kennel. Locking the tailgate back in place, he scratched his unshaven chin and slid back into the driver's seat of his truck, not caring to notice that his jacket held a fresh layer of mud he had picked up when brushing against the side of the truck.

The clutch slipped and made a grinding noise as he wrestled it into gear. When he pulled out of the middle of the three bays at the dump, he passed at least a dozen other vehicles waiting to unload their own debris.

Figuring he might as well change the oil, he stopped at a local auto parts store, noticing a 'help wanted' sign on the door. The youthful gray-haired woman who greeted him was an unfamiliar face.

"Ted around?" he grunted without looking up, walking down one of the aisles before she could respond, before returning to plop several quarts of oil on the counter.

"That'll be $34.95," the woman said quietly.

"Ain't seen you around here before," Gaston said, passing the necessary greenbacks across the counter. "What happened to old Ted?"

"He passed away last fall," she answered, handing him the receipt. "I need to find someone to help run the business. He took care of all that and now…"

Changing the subject, she looked at Gaston and asked, "Know anyone?"

"You a relative or somethin'?" Gaston said, squinting as he spoke.

"I'm Ted's wife," she answered.

"Sorry ma'am. Didn't know Ted was married."

Picking up the box that held the cans of oil, he walked out toward the door before turning back as he elbowed it open.

"Sorry about Ted. I'll ask around to see if anyone's lookin' for work".

Gaston shoved the box of oil cans into the pickup bed and slammed the tailgate shut, wondering what had killed old Ted and how he had kept such a fine looking wife hidden from view. Later, when Eel stopped by with a couple of fresh fish, Gaston asked him about Ted.

He learned that Ted had died of cancer in October, leaving behind his wife of forty years. Eel said her name was Katherine and that she had stayed quietly behind the scenes managing the finances of the business. By all accounts, Katherine and Ted had accrued a considerable nest egg and had been planning to retire to Hawaii when Ted's illness struck. With no children to help with the business, it had fallen on Katherine to manage both the books and the inventory.

"They had a wonderful life together," Eel told Gaston. "Sad it had to end this way."

A week or so later, Gaston stopped into the store again, this time for an air filter and a new bulb for the rear taillight that had burned out God knows when. Leaning across the counter to look through the catalog of parts with Katherine, he noticed how sweet she smelled and how gentle her hands looked as they thumbed through the pages.

It wasn't the first time he had regretted acting like a jerk. Ever since Angelina had died, he found the occasions to be short and abrupt with people ever present. This time, though, he felt unusually sheepish at having been brusque with someone as vulnerable as a recent widow like Katherine.

"Look, ma'am," he said after locating the number for the part he needed. "I want to apologize for my attitude the other day. I hadn't heard about Ted and I sure as sunrise never knew he had a wife."

Gaston started stumbling on his words as Katherine walked to the bin to get the bulb he needed.

"What I'd like to say…what I'd like to do in the way of apology, is to help you out here in the store till you can find somebody permanent."

Katherine stopped in her tracks and looked at Gaston.

"I'd appreciate the help, Mr. Noel. I'll pay you

biweekly at $2 above the going wage, but I'm sorry to tell you that I can't offer any benefits at the moment. You can start tomorrow at opening. Any crossness with the customers and I'll thank you to leave on your own, because it won't be tolerated here."

"I'll see you tomorrow at 10AM sharp," Gaston replied, unsure of why he suddenly relished being ordered around by a woman.

"Ten sharp it is," Katherine replied before walking to the back, leaving Gaston standing alone in the store.

Chapter Twelve
Merciful Time

After the long Alaska winter and just when a person might think that life has become a hard-edged annoyance, spring bursts forth. By May there is more light than not, and winter's jaded attitudes are quickly replaced with the perspective that new energy brings. It is almost as if a new chapter in life has begun. The survival of the dismal darkness and long, empty days gives way to hope for easier times, as Alaskans emerge from their homes and begin to tackle living with enthusiasm again.

All along the Kenai Peninsula, signs of life return as bears come out of hibernation, ice melts from the rivers and eagle's nests sport the downy heads of newborn chicks. The sounds of running water, chirping birds, the din of moving vehicles and people's voices replace winter's quiet. The leaves, at first tiny mouse-ears in size, now umbrella the earth and wildflowers sprout almost overnight in the nurturing sun. The air, fresh with newness, still holds the nights chill. Soon, the ocean breezes of summer will bathe the southern Kenai Peninsula in the comfort of a new Alaska summer.

As June arrived, Gaston continued his job at the parts store. Somehow, Katherine had never found another employee and somehow, Gaston didn't seem to mind. As a matter of fact, he was well underway toward meeting their mutual goal of replacing the old manual parts cataloging system with a state of the art computer program that would allow them to serve the customers faster while simultaneously updating both the inventory and the balance sheets.

He was close to settling the insurance claim on the *Angelina* and he had even finally made it over to have dinner with Eel and Ella Jo, surprising them when he brought Katherine along with him. The four of them got along well, and more dinners followed, often ending with Ella Jo and Katherine working on projects while Eel helped Gaston draw up plans for the new seiner he was preparing to order from a shipbuilder in Seattle.

During the week, Gaston would often make runs up to Soldotna or Anchorage to pick up supplies for either the new computer system or for making repairs around the store. He had driven past the eagles nest at milepost 139.5 so many times that he used it as a marker for how much longer he had to get to his destination. It was good to see the nest inhabited—and so close to the highway, too. It was too high for him to count the number of chicks inside, but he knew there were at least two.

One day, cruising along on a particularly beautiful day, he glanced up at the nest as usual only to be startled by the whoosh of an eagle darting by only inches in front of his windshield. Reflexly, he jammed his foot on the brakes and swerved, veer-

Chapter 12—Merciful Time

ing over into the oncoming lane before slowing to a stop on the shoulder of his own side of the road.

He heard the eagle land on his roof as he sat there regaining his composure. Through the glass of the sunroof, he could see the bird's white tail feathers and part of its back.

"What the…" he sputtered, starting to open the door.

The movement startled the eagle into lifting its wings and hopping sideways on the roof, which prompted Gaston to stay in the truck for now. Looking up through the sunroof again, he could hardly believe what he saw. It was an eagle for sure and a large one at that. The dark feathers were a blend of tobacco brown, black and midnight blue interspersed with highlights of gray that gave the bird an overall dark, almost black appearance. The head was white and the eyes yellow, the beak and feet a golden shade of yellow and the talons—long, sleek and shiny black. But what shocked Gaston and made him sink back into his seat in disbelief was the white patch on the eagle's leg.

"It's you," he said simply.

Hali flew back up to the nest, which was about twenty feet back from where Gaston was parked. Gaston watched Hali hold his wings out and hover near the edge while another eagle scooted sideways in the nest, before Hali eventually landed beside her. He thought it looked like the same one that he had seen with the one who had inhabited his crow's nest. In front of them, he could see the baby chicks' heads bobbing up and down.

Gaston shook his head slowly and wiped away the tears that had formed in his eyes before looking up again, this time making eye contact with Hali. Here in this moment, everything rushed back into his consciousness—the death of his own mate, the loss of his men at sea, the sinking of the *Angelina*, his advancing age, his ornery knee…his immense loneliness. There, standing on the edge of the highway, looking at Hali and Lyra, he cried the tears he had held inside for so long. Cars whizzed by at regular intervals, but no one stopped or seemed to notice the broken man now sitting, spent and empty in his truck.

The sun was setting behind Augustine Volcano across Cook Inlet when Gaston decided he was ready to go home. Hali had flown off for now, but Lyra and the chicks stayed in the nest. Gaston stood on his running board and nodded at them, pulling his lips into a wobbly half smile as he did, before getting back inside his truck. He could see Hali in the distance returning, and that was enough to know. He turned the key in the ignition and drove off, making a U-turn on the highway to head back home. Once back in Homer, he left a note on the rear door to the store to let Katherine know he was back.

Tonight Gaston would let Rufer sleep indoors and he would even share his dinner with the dog who had so quietly shared his life for the past nine years. He fell asleep early with the TV still running, waking up about midnight to turn it off before falling into a deep and restful sleep.

Chapter Thirteen
Seattle

Experiencing an Alaska summer is most humbling. Seldom in modern America is there an opportunity for the average person to engage in such an intimate connection with the earth.

On the Kenai Peninsula, far from the urban center of Anchorage, nature still manages to reign supreme in spite of the influx of thousands of visitors to its rivers and shores. How easily man blends in with the lifecycles of nature. Bears, fishing openly for salmon, actively store fat before their long winter's hibernation. Salmon spawning in rivers that take them to the tiniest, most shallow threads of water, lay their eggs before leaving their life to the next generation; all while humans move among them.

For those who live on the Kenai Peninsula year round, summer is a time to fill their freezers with fish and game that will help feed their families through the winter. It is a time to repair the worn roofs, build the new additions, shore up the broken fences and undertake whatever other repairs the nine months of winter have left. It is a time to stock up on supplies and prepare summer toys for storage—for fall will be brief and winter will be sudden, and it is best to be ready when it comes.

As soon as the daylight peaks in June, it begins to shrink once more, until by December the darkness has fully returned. Alaskans know this and live with this and understand that summer is but a glimpse of heaven that spurs them to make the best of life that can be. As they work hard, so too do they play hard, all the while preparing for the cycle to begin once again.

No one except Gaston was surprised when he and Katherine married late in August. In spite of the fact that she said she would have no part in marrying a man who spent half his life at sea, she happily took her new husband's arm as the two walked out of the courthouse with Eel and Ella Jo right behind.

Gaston held Katherine's arm tightly to his, tucking her hand inside his as they walked. A year ago about this time, he could never have imagined he would be here now; nor that instead of barking orders at Eel, his loyal friend would be serving as the best man at the wedding he never then could have foreseen.

Their reception was small, but all that the two of them hoped it could be. Gaston's neighbors, Bob and Betty, Eel and Ella Jo and their sons Ben and Jess and daughter JamiJoelle all joined them. Everyone laughed as they gathered around a fire pit on the beach well into the night. Ben and Jess both played fiddle and Ben's fiancée, Shera, played dulcimer, making for a lively evening of dancing and laughter and fun.

A steady stream of locals came by, most bringing fish or dishes to pass to feed the growing crowd. Before the setting sun, Fr. John Mac blessed the new couple and their lives—a gesture that touched both Gaston and Katherine, neither of whom were members of his church. Gaston shook Eel's pastor's hand and handed him a beer, then turned up a piece of log for him to sit on so he could join the festivities. Others did likewise, pulling up driftwood logs or throwing tarps on the beach to join in the celebration that carried music well into the night.

Before everyone went home, Gaston and Katherine presented Eel and Ella Jo with two tickets to Seattle, along with an invitation to join them there early next month for what they were told was another celebration of both the marriage and of Eel and Gaston's survival at sea. The four of them, Gaston told them, would then return to Alaska on the brand new seiner, the *Angelina II*.

Over the next week, Gaston finished arrangements for both the trip to Seattle and the final payment on the *Angelina II*. His boat had been well insured, and even though investigating officials had determined that the loss of the two crewman at sea was an unavoidable accident, Gaston sent off checks for a generous amount of money to the families of the two crewman who would never come home again. He also made a substantial donation to the Coast Guard relief fund in gratitude for the sensational rescue that had saved him and Eel but that had cost them three of their own in the process.

On September 9, Gaston, Katherine, Eel and Ella Jo were standing on the dock north of Seattle preparing to board the beautiful new seiner, *Angelina II,* their week at a luxury hotel now over. As Katherine and Ella Jo walked up the gangway and began to tour the cabin, Eel and Gaston walked alongside the new seiner on the docks, marveling at the fine boat before them.

"She's as proud a mistress o' the sea as a man could ever hope for," Eel exclaimed.

"That she is," Gaston answered, before bringing Eel to the bow to show him the surprise.

Looking up at the bow, Gaston pointed to the long plaque that was attached above the name *Angelina II*. Unlike the rest of the boards that were shiny and new, the plaque was weathered and worn, jagged at one end and bearing the first five letters of the new boat's predecessor. It was the only surviving piece of the Angelina left after she sank, making the part of the name that had been left unscathed—*Angel*—all the more meaningful to the two men.

"It's as proud a tribute as could be made, Cap'n," Eel said somberly.

The trip north alongside Canada and across the Gulf of Alaska was as peaceful and uneventful as any Gaston had ever made. Even Katherine seemed to embrace life at sea, much to the surprise of her new husband. The last night of the journey, the four guided the *Angelina II* into the Emerald Cove. It was as beautiful as Gaston remembered it and as calm as it had been the night he and Eel first anchored there one year ago. There were even a couple of eagles soaring overhead, but Gaston did not recognize them as the two who had done so much to help save him and Eel.

With some trepidation, the two men decided to take the skiff over to the beach, insisting that their wives come with them. With even more trepidation, they stepped out onto the beach from which they once thought they would never leave. Walking along the gravel, they located the rock that once held the only fresh water supply they had known there. It was hard to believe that the tiny depression in the top had held enough water to keep them alive.

Eel found a shred of blue polytarp sticking out from underneath a rock and tucked it into his pocket. Somehow the simple memento reminded him of how lucky he was to be standing here today. This time, though, the sea was calm and the air warm. On the way back to the skiff, Gaston stopped to look at something he saw laying on the beach.

"Eel. C'mere!" He called, trying not to let his voice betray the rush of emotion he felt.

Before he could speak again, Eel saw it, too. It

was waterlogged and weathered from a year of being battered by the sea, but there on the beach before them, was the rest of the plank that had borne the name of the *Angelina* on its side. Eel picked it up and handed it to Gaston. "Here, Cap'n. I know what this means to you."

Gaston ran his fingers along the swollen wood, staring at the splintered left edge and down across the letters ...*ina* before letting his fingers slip off the far end. Tucking the piece of wood under his arm, he walked silently back to the skiff where Katherine and Ella Jo were already waiting. He showed it to them while Eel explained, but no one but the two men could really understand the importance of the find.

Unlike a year ago, there was no storm that night and everyone slept well. The *Angelina II* slid quietly into Homer Harbor the next afternoon, and tied up at the slip that Gaston had kept rented for the past year. The four, exhausted from the long journey, went back to Gaston's cabin to sleep. In the morning they would unload their gear.

Chapter Fourteen
The Power of Love

By late September and into October, a few eagles begin returning to the spit. By December, they are as plentiful as the rafts of sea otters that move into Mud Bay on the east side of the thin landmass that personifies Homer.

About this time, the last of the RVers disappear, as do the recreational boaters, many of who will return next March for the Winter King Salmon tournament that kicks off a new boating season.

In the fall, the numerous boardwalk shops along the spit are boarded up. With no real attraction for tourists, the spit becomes a much quieter place where locals can enjoy the solitude of impending winter. In spite of the cold and looming darkness, surfers in dry suits will soon tackle the large waves of the winter storms while locals ride their horses on the beaches and people just generally gather to do things like watch the ferry come in from Kodiak or Seldovia or even points far beyond.

Soon, the harbor will be full of ice and maybe an occasional sea lion will move in. But that is winter, and right now it is still fall.

Gaston and Eel had been up to the cabin and

were on their way back to the docks by sunrise the day after their return from the Emerald Cove. The low tide forced them to look down as they walked the ramp to the floats, not noticing until they were almost to the boat that there were four eagles sitting on the edge of the crow's nest of the *Angelina II*. Gaston recognized one of them as the same eagle that had helped him and Eel after the sinking at the Emerald Cove. Two of the birds were immature and retained the dark coloring of youth. The fourth one looked like the same eagle that had been sitting in the nest that day that Gaston had stopped along the highway.

Shaking his head, Gaston tried to hide the smile that was threatening to creep across is face.

"Looks like our two friends from the Emerald Cove have started a family."

"Never thought four of 'em would fit in a crow's nest like that," Eel answered, looking sideways up and squinting into the bright sun to see them.

"Looks like they're your problem now, Captain," Gaston said.

'What's that, Cap'n?" Eel said, not sure he had understood.

"I said, looks like they're your problem now, Captain." With that, Gaston handed a manila envelope to Eel, who stared without speaking.

"It's all in there, "Gaston continued. "The title—you'll have to register it in your own name, of course —I couldn't do that for you…"

Eel looked inside the envelope and saw the reg-

Chapter 14—The Power of Love

istration papers. Lifting them out, he saw the vessel name, *Angelina II* and the owner's name—Jameson Andrew Jones—written on the form.

Eel could still not find words and fought to hold back tears.

"T'ain't no need for you to say nothin', my friend," Gaston said, choking back his own tears. "T'ain't no need at all."

For several minutes, the two men stood there as a brisk wind slapped a rope that loosely anchored the skiff to the *Angelina II*.

It was Eel who spoke first.

"Cap'n…" he began slowly, "You don't need to do this… you don't owe me nothin'…nothin', Cap'n…nothin' like this."

"Never said I owed you anything, Eel," Gaston replied. "T'ain't about owin'…T'ain't about nothin' but me handin' over my place on the sea to the best skipper a man could know."

Eel shook his head slowly in disbelief and then walked up to the *Angelina II* and ran his hand slowly along her side. A couple of times he hesitated, letting the smoothness of her finish absorb into his senses. Even in the brisk wind, her thick, planked sides felt warmed from the sun. When he reached the bow where the plank from the original *Angelina* had been nailed in place, he ran his hands—first one and then the other—over the word *Angel*, letting it slip off the raised edge where the rest of her name had been torn away in the storm.

"I'd like to keep the other part of that plank,"

Gaston said, "The ending to her name...I'd like to keep that."

"Wouldn't have it no other way, Cap'n," Eel responded.

"She'll always be a part of me..." Gaston, unable to finish the sentence, bowed his head.

A thick fog blown in by the wind enveloped the two men as they stood there. It comforted them and gave them time to reconcile their emotions. It soothed them and embraced them as it absorbed their tears. In the stillness, a distant bell clanged as its vessel tossed in the harbor.

Chapter 14—The Power of Love

Gaston walked slowly away, leaving the new Captain of the *Angelina II* with his boat.

"She's got a good set a lights on her…and state of the art radar…Hell, she's even got a danged GPS, Eel," he called back. "Fog like this ain't gonna never be a problem to you again."

Gaston heard the first splash in the water beside him as he walked, followed in quick succession by three more as Hali, Lyra and their two offspring dove for fish in the water beside the dock; knowing, as they did, that everything had turned out just the way destiny had determined it would.

www.ingramcontent.com/pod-product-compliance
Lightning Source LLC
Chambersburg PA
CBHW060846050426
42453CB00008B/857